chapter one:
What Are girls and Boys? 4
chapter two:
not ALL Boys Are useless! 10
chapter three:
Boys Are stupid 18
chapter four:
Fun With Boys! 32
chapter five:
Boys make good pets 40
chapter six:
Boyfriends Are stupid 46
chapter seven:
Break-up Fun! 56
chapter eight:
Training a Boyfriend 66

"don't put a cat
on your head—
it hurts real bad!"

Chapter one:

What are girls and boys?

Girls are bundles of joy and gifts from heaven.

boys pick their nose in front of 7-eleven!

girls are made of sugar and
spice and everything nice.

boys are made of boogers, cooties, and head lice.

girls smell sweet like fresh-cut flowers.

boys smell like doodie...

and never take showers!

chapter two:

not all boys are useless!

some boys have unique talents and contribute great things to society.

some can actually read!

(picture books, of course)

cheesy plug

some are great chefs!
"I make cottage cheese by letting the milk go bad."
milk
expires 1984
"mmm-
mmm-
GOOD!"

Some are great musicians!
"I can fart the Star-Spangled banner in less than 30 seconds!"
pfft pfft pfft pfft

some are great poets!

"Roses are red,
violets are blue,
oh crap!
I have gum
on my shoe!"

Some are great singers!

"I can burp the alphabet without taking a breath!"

some are great improvisers!
"once i ran out of toilet paper and had to use my hand!"
Tip: never hold hands with a boy!

Some make great politicians!
"I vote we have Twinkies and snow cones for lunch everyday!"

OK, we lied!
all
boys
are
pretty much useless!

chapter three:

Boys are Stupid

Fact:
thinking can be dangerous!
Ouch!
ideas make boys' heads hurt!

how to make a quick 5 bucks off a boy!

girl: do you have six $5s for a $20?

boy: i only have five $5s!

girl: ok you can owe me $5 later.

boy: ok! (to himself: sucker!)

it's like taking candy from a baby!

game show!
(for all you boys playing at home: F is not the correct answer!)
Q: What is the capital of Florida?
-200,000
300
500,000
'F'
tallahassee

obviously, boys were not in line when they handed out brains!

F.Y.I. remember what "boy" means: (born only yesterday)

a few things boys are better at than girls:

1: armpit farting
2: belching words
3: flicking boogers for field goals
4: spitting in air and trying to catch it
5: scarfing down food without breathing
6: eating bugs
7: picking scabs
8: making bubbles in the bathtub

how come boys don't ask for directions?

girl: i think we're lost.
boy: we're not lost.
girl: maybe we should ask for directions....
boy: we don't need help.

girl: but i've seen that house 10 times!

boy: that's my house.

girl: isn't that where we are going??

boy: ok, we're here! told you we didn't need help.

hint: if lost, don't ask another boy for directions... he's probably lost too!

Why is it, the smellier a boy's **fart**...
the **Prouder** he is!?

things he might say after the great accomplishment:

"that was my big bertha!"

"is someone baking brownies?"

"silent, but deadly!"

"you smelt it, you dealt it!"

"did someone sit on a duck?"

Philosophy:
is this glass half-full or half-empty?
...2 hours later:
"i'm thirsty! can i drink it now?"
q: if a tree fell on a boy in the woods... would anyone hear it?
a: who cares!

did you know?
boys eat yellow snow
tip:
boys...if you mix
dirt with water you
get chocolate milk!

Why don't boys brush their teeth?
because it wouldn't taste good with the worms they just ate!
YUCK!

other ways boys use toothpaste:

1: glue. 2: hair gel.

3: put on zits!

4: clean their ears.

5: midafternoon snack.

6: squirt each other in the eye.

TOOTHPASTE

chapter four:

FUN WITH BOYS!

do something like this....

girl: i'm SO mad at YOU!

boy-you-barely-know: what's wrong?

girl: well, if you don't know then you'll never understand!

(now walk away....)

...or talk in secret code

communicate in complete secrecy in front of boys!

(it's called spelling!)

it works like this...

girl 1: t-o-d-d i-s a d-o-r-k.

girl 2: t-o-t-a-l-l-y.

only girls understand this secret language!

...or give them a math quiz!

nature fun!

take a boy on a nature walk.
go deep into the woods.
tell him to close his eyes
and count to 100.

run away!

birdie!
birdie!

...or dress up a boy
you'll be amazed!
boys make really ugly girls!
hint:
take lots of pictures for future blackmailing!

reality check:
Types of boys:
pig
dog
jackass
Pick one.

take this quiz!

what is the difference between boys and dogs?

a: one has fleas
b: one poops in the yard
c: one sniffs butts
d: one sleeps all day
e: one smells

take your time, this is a tough one.

OK that was a trick question!

there is no difference between

boys
and
dogs!

now fetch me the paper, boy!

Chapter Five:

Boys make good Pets

only feed a boy twice a day.

hint: always wash behind a boy's ears...

this is where they hide boogers and toenails for future snacking!

reminder:
B.F.F.
take him out to potty
20 minutes
after mealtime!

there is a reason why boys have separate bathrooms!

scratch here to find out why

Danger

smelling this can be hazardous to your health!

ha! ha!

if you smelled this you are as stupid as a boy...

girls: please start over from page 1!

boys: continue looking at the pretty pictures!

Put down newspapers!

boys: this is not a swimming pool!
or a shower!
boys...
that little handle
is to flush the toilet.
...it's not for decoration!

Chapter six:

Boyfriends are stupid

why waste money on a cab?
there's always
public transportation!

what not to expect from a boy on a date:

1. hold your door open
2. pay for dinner
3. eat with utensils
4. not farting or belching the entire time
5. kiss you goodnight (this is a good thing—trust me!)
6. call you again

Phone rules!
do NOT
wait by the
phone for
him to call!
most likely
he doesn't
even know
how to
use a phone!
hello?

be afraid if your boyfriend...
a. has more shoes than you.
b. has bathroom products more expensive than yours.
c. is on a fad diet!
slim quick
d. knows what kind of jeans you're wearing.
are those david & goliath?

and be super-duper afraid if you catch him wearing your panties!
"I feel sexy!"

boy decoder:

(check the box if you have heard this before.)

- it's not you, it's me. ☐
- i love you, but i'm not in love with you. ☐
- you deserve someone better. ☐
- i need some space. ☐
- i don't wanna ruin our friendship. ☐

all mean the same thing...

i'm too chicken to tell you,

but...

i don't like you anymore and i want to date your friend with big boobs!

what kind of girlfriend are you?

take this quiz!

let's say your boyfriend tried to kiss your best friend. would you....

a. blame yourself!

"it's my fault!"

"i'm too fat!"

"i'm not cute enough!"

b. make him cry!

c. kiss his best friend!

*if you answered a... close this book and hit yourself on the head with it!

chapter seven:

Break-Up Fun!

the best way to break up with a **boy** is to pretend you don't know him.

Wanna watch me play a video game?
Sorry, i don't talk to strangers!

sometimes a boy won't accept the fact that it's over.

be more direct!
rock
throw!

maybe he still doesn't get it!
"I love you, my little buttercup"

maybe he says,
"don't leave me or i'll die!"

that's when a girl must do the meanest, cruelest, most awful thing a girl can do...

make him someone else's problem!

1: find a really dumb blonde girl.

2: introduce her to your stupid boyfriend.

3: run away!

if necessary, change your name and start wearing a disguise!

hee hee hee

I'M WITH STUPID

if all else fails, use the silent treatment...
this drives boys nuts!

"speak to the hand."

"la la la"
"i'm sorry! can i take
you to dinner? can i buy you
a new outfit? anything!
please say something!!"

chapter eight:

training a Boyfriend

if for some stupid reason you decide to keep a boyfriend...

it's your job to train him!

"I just wanted some cheese!"

etiquette:

hint: boys...the pointy pronglike utensil on the left side of the plate is a fork (the left side is that-a-way ←)!

a fork is NOT to be used for....
1: stabbing bugs.
2: sword-fighting with other stupid boys.
3: sticking up nose for booger excavation.
4: scratching butts.

just a friendly reminder...
Oops!
* don't let a boy sit on your couch unless the plastic cover is on!
boys aren't house-broken!

boys can't accessorize!
"like
that
bag was
so
last"
year!

always check a boy before he leaves the house:

1: make sure he zips his fly.

2: make sure his socks match.

3: make sure he has on clean underwear.

4: make sure his shoes are on the correct feet.

5: make sure he's wearing pants!

and make sure under no circumstances whatsoever... that a boy does laundry!

Sucker

a boyfriend is **not** allowed to:

spit!!!

fart in the car!

belch in front of your parents!

follow you into the bathroom!

make you pull his finger!

put you in a headlock!

put empty containers back in the fridge!

dress himself!

cut his own hair!

give you a nickname!

watch more than four hours of football in a day!

and last but not least....

act like he knows you in public!

major rule!

when you're telling him a problem, a boyfriend is **not** allowed to interrupt and tell you his opinion before you have even told him what the problem is!

"new rule" rule:

new rules may be invented **on the spot** and be retroactive.

and if he breaks the rules...

just remember: for every

stupid smelly cootie-ridden boy:

there is a rock.

boys are stupid,
and they make me wanna throw up!
throw rocks at them!
by todd harris goldman
workman publishing • new york

i dedicate this book to my parents...
(or at least they tell me they're my parents)
david and leni goldman, for putting up with
my silliness for all these years, making whoopie,
and creating such a stupid, smelly boy!

 Published simultaneously in Canada by Thomas Allen & Son, Limited.

Library of Congress Cataloging-in-Publication Data is available.

ISBN-13: 978-0-7611-3593-7

Workman books are available at special discounts when purchased in bulk for premiums and sales promotions as well as for fund-raising or educational use. Special editions or book excerpts can also be created to specification. For details, contact the Special Sales Director at the address below.

Workman Publishing Company, Inc.
225 Varick Street
New York, NY 10014-4381
www.workman.com

Printed in China
First printing March 2005

10 9 8